MUSH

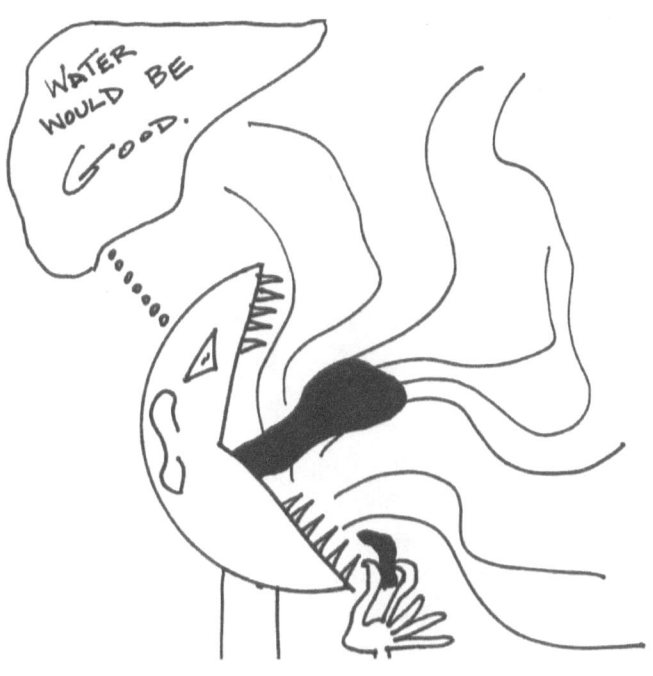

Poems by Brett Lars Underwood

Kansas City Spartan Press Missouri

Spartan Press
Kansas City, Missouri
spartanpresskc.com

Copyright (c) Brett Underwood 2018
First Edition 1 3 5 7 9 10 8 6 4 2
ISBN: 978-1-946642-39-4
LCCN: 2017964753

Design, edits and layout: Jason Ryberg
Cover art: Jerome Gaynor
Author photo: Jim McGowin
All rights reserved. No part of this publication may be reproduced or transmitted in any form or by any means, electronic or mechanical, including photocopying, recording or by info retrieval system, without prior written permission from the author.

Spartan Press would like to thank Prospero's Books, The Fellowship of N-finite Jest, The Prospero Institute of Disquieted P/o/e/t/i/c/s, Will Leathem, Tom Wayne, Jeanette Powers, j.d.tulloch, Jon Bidwell, Jason Preu, Mark McClane, Tony Hayden and the whole Osage Arts Community.

Work is a Four-Letter Word first appeared on *52ndcity.com*, *Sometimes I Work in a Grandiose Castle* first appeared in *FLOOD STAGE An Anthology of Saint Louis Poets*

CONTENTS

Philosophy End / 1

Ready for Lift Off / 3

Work is a Four-Letter Word / 9

Word is a Four-Letter Word / 18

Ablutions / 23

Creep / 25

Kleenex / 33

Man's Crisis of Identity / 35

Wagon Wheel Cities are Annoying / 38

Astro Pig / 40

Spin Cycle / 41

Messy and Complicated and Riddled
  with Hypocrisy / 42

Physics / 46

Go Soothingly on the Grease Mud / 48

To You, Cloudy Girl / 52

Sometimes I Work in a Grandiose Castle / 54

Headbutt Baby / 59

Vision or … / 64

Slick / 66

The Chainsaw Says Get Up! / 68

Out of the Tree / 70

To my father, the original writer in my life,
Larry D. Underwood and my mother,
Beverly Sue Underwood.

*Beware Those Quick to Censure:
They Are Afraid of What They Do
Not Know*

*Beware Those Who Seek Constant
Crowds; They Are Nothing
Alone*
          -Charles Bukowski

Philosophy End

Remember, if you can, a message shot
to you like a diamond bullet:
When attempting to lasso boomerangs,
cowboys always lose when trying
to administer inoculations in a jungle
of beings willing to shoot wisdom
into the hearts of children and idiots.

Idiots always lose when trying
to administer inoculations in a town
of beings willing to shoot wisdom
into the hearts of children and cowboys.

Children when they got a boomerang
are going to get hit in the head
and lose at trying
to administer inoculations in a bouncy
house built by children slaves
and pumped up with a gasoline-powered
generator.

But they   is   there   now, next to me in traffic;
slumped over in their junker;

What?????

But they are wearing sun glasses
and you can hear 80s punk
and you don't know whether it is theirs
Or yours,
AND
Nice ride!!!!
AND
You're O.K. 'til they find the body
You're O.K. 'til they find the mind
AND
You're O.K. 'til they find the body
You're O.K. 'til you've lost your mind.

Ready for Lift Off

Take your wait off
Strap your wings on

Gotta get away from you Cretins!
Flying higher and higher

While faceless slaves
feed the beast
Grow, slaughter, cook and serve
the feast

Sew the walkabout threads
stripped from wheels
Spin willy-nilly wobbly heels
Shuffle feet
Scuttle butt
Talking the talk
Walking the walk
Clod-kickin' nomads
Riddling clichés
In piecemeal-economic class
majority of days
Knotting and tangling
Screaming and steaming
Angels falling in teams

Coaxing hope from men and children
Suffering guilt and schemes
for flavored vodka
to put out the flames.

Faceless in frenzied crowds
not their piglets for a tit
Sweet silk web of perks
Splinters in their lips

It's a wooden cow
Eating the genius grass of now
Leisurely-gone-mechanical
Madness habit
Horses clip-clopping through the sky,
Hot on the trail of a giant carrot,
Bobbing
On the end of a string
Tied to a stick unseen.
Burning spear becomes the sun.

Sorry.
Pardon me.
Sodomy
Crying in reality
Steeping in normality
Buttheads are bound
to butt heads
that buy shit, bite shits

Bytes hit and heights hit
won't give the satisfaction of
the real tail hit.

You chop down peasant trees
if you can't get no
pleasantries?
You a pissant?
Pissed off, beaten down?
Disinegratefully muttering,
Icarus is sick of us clowns

And the sin of Pomegranate
Sultans of Homer
Keeping her down under
while up top
behemoth, violent women
with bushels and bushels of rags
and frenetic mongrels dropped
from hot snatches
to scamper about floors of life
'cause they were lonely.
Heel Scream Bitch Moan
Retort cranked to 9

The locked-down boom box blares
Soft-rock soma static
Statistician death

Equation of chaos avoidance.

See its nonsense?

Others anguish
Sitting in the John Wilkes Booth
with the Donner Party
and no gold

Sorry utter ranting of wishwash blather
of too much peroxide
silicone and the glide
and the kind of salvation
they sell on late-night television.

Faces cracked and exploding,
But you tip
a little extra
so the waitress
can shoot it between her toes
tonight.

Gotta get high tonight
Outta sight
Set a course for the midnight light
Window-pained souls squeegee a play of rage
Turn to stone in its chemical cage
Jaws yawning uncertainty
Future doom cult in dreads circle spirits
Their wagons around teepees

Snap and rage
against bludgeoning
the right
Clothes tumble in the drier thoughts
fall in sync

Scattered and disconnected,
but all feeling the same heat.

Stop the car!
I'm getting' out.
I can't take it!
Hey lOOk out.
There's somebody comin'
And there's nothing you can do about it!!!

That's O.K.
He ain't got long to go
So we'll forgive him.

Something spontaneous
Possibly dangerous
Something precarious
Probably not legal
Something fun
Eventually lethal
But we probably won't be out
That long.

Ride it on a glide like that
Let it prove its groove
Slow down ancient mellow day
and play it to the moon

And now we hurtle through the stars
The President says we goin' to Mars!
Just to get away from this rubbish heap!
Flying Higher and higher
Until we drown in melted glaciers.
…another failed attempt at escape
From Cretins and their addiction
To the glug glug.

Work is a Four-Letter Word

Work is a four-letter word.
(So is word, though.)
Does it seem like you're working more than ever?
Ha Ha.
Not according to the statistics, I'm afraid.
It may seem like we are all busy as ever,
but statistics show
something different.
Or do they?
What constitutes work?
Cube is short for cubicle.
Working
Business
Busy-ness
Occupation
A drought of leisure is a threat to
public health,
personal health,
mental health,
physical health.
He's at the office.
Two-car garage.
Mortgage.
Footpounds.
Desired effect?

Do you work so much you don't know what to do?
Solitaire.
Boxlunch.
Pesticide.
Occupational hazards include back injuries.
Carpal tunnel syndrome.
You have to really be repetitive to get a syndrome.
Or maybe you'll just chafe.
Jogger's nipple.
Not listed are other more severe maladies.
I'm at work
I can't. I have to work
You're going to be late for work.
I'll meet you after work
Why work?
Sleeping pills.
These bills are getting me down.
I can't pay my bills.
I spend my free time shopping.
Day care.
I can't. I have to work in the morning.
I better not. I should work.
You missed work.
Why weren't you at work?
I'm looking for work.
You better get to work.
Men at Work, of course. (Ha, ha …)
Pistol in mouth.

Armani suit.
Trophy wife.
They took the busboy home and ...
Ass kisser.
All work and no play makes Jack a dull boy.
Recreational drugs vs. the memory of work.
Working for the weekend (everybody is, ya' know!)
Ouch.
Oh, and whistle while you work (yeah, that's fucking cute ... straight from the oppressor.
Is that what Walt Disney was doing there?)
Plastic forks and spoons.
What are you working on?
Will this work? (no, but it might fit ... lemme see. Oooh! Did that hurt?)
We can work it out (not without a hammer to smash that inner radio!)
Would you two like to work together?
Let's work on it.
Cluster fuck.
But the evil little demon is there inside the heads who squawk, *What do you do?*
What the fuck are you doing?!!!
Constant evaluations
decline in autonomy
white lies
Warm bath, sharp razor.
Mocca.

Insubordination.
Suck up to the boss.
Cause and effect.
I can't stand it, he just sleeps all day and then goes to work.
He told me I had a *protestant work ethic*.
Phphphphff!
I'm not even religious!
Pyramid scheme.
Thorstein Veblen wrote *The Theory of the Working Class*
You can buy it at WalMart.
Malnutrition.
Welfare.
Put your back into it, College Boy!
The American Dream.
What are you?
How do you make money?
I know, I know, it has become human nature these days.
Everyone is too fucking busy to know what's going on.
I can't smell the flowers. I'm allergic.
Take a pill.
Do you have an over-riding feeling of being rushed?
Xanax.
Prozac.
Oprah.
Thought criminal.
His commute to work is three hours each way.
She skateboards to work on Thursdays.
I like to ride the bus to work.

My Mom smokes a jibber when she's driving me to work.
The boss got a DWI on the way to work.
We fucked off all day.
Flippin' buggers ... er, uh, I mean burgers, Sir.
Bored people are boring.
Twenty car pileup.
There is little or no leisure in American culture.
We are all left to wonder how the next guy
gets by
or if we can ride on his coat tails without him
catching on.
Lottery ticket.
I work during the day.
I work at night.
I'm working the third shift.
I'm working on it.
I've got to start working out.
Do you work out?
Slots.
Let me work those numbers up for you?
She's at work 'till ten. Come on over.
I don't know. Working, I guess.
He's doing this babe from work?
She worked her way up the ladder.
We went to her work party.
White Zin.
Traffic copter.
That'll work!

He fell off a ladder at work.
Don't walk under that ladder, Rookie, screamed
the foreman.
They call me the working man.
Joe six-pack.
Women's undergarments.
Hee hee.
Devoted family man.
Lawn.
Urban sprawl.
Working America.
Working the crowd.
Work it, Baby!
What time do you get off work?
How does that work?
I don't know how she makes it work.
I don't know how he made it to work.
It's in the works.
He works in the arts.
Where did those lepers work?
My moms used to go to work at the five-and-dime.
It is workable.
Fuckin' Commie!
He sings for a living, Jackson does.
He goes, *I wanna be a happy idiot.*
Working for the legal tender,
she said at the water cooler.
Tony smells like toner.

Eating disorder.
The *N* word.
She works in the fields 12 hours a day.
Ugh, she smells like dirt.
She is the salt of the Earth.
He works as a preventative maintenance supervisor to the Imp.
I work at home.
I have homework to finish up.
Bored at work?
Office Humor to entertain you while you work.
Not while I work!
Jenny really worked on her abs.
Work is a scalar quantity,
but it can be positive or negative.
I would like to improve my work confidence.
Wasting time at work …
He sleeps in the shitter at work.
He nodded off with a needle in his arm at work.
The power of play at work.
You're a joy to work with.
She sells seashells down by the seashore.
Before he hit it big, he sold his ass on the streets.
Job.
Work in Texas.
Sleep Disorder.
Low-priced work gear

She left him. He was out of work.
Facial tic.
I have to buy some new work boots.
Ergonomic chairs.
Whip cracker.
He's never had a job in his life.
I have to wear a work uniform despite the shrinking job market.
What twit designed this work station?
Work more, fuck less.
When money goes out the door,
love goes out the window.
He travels a lot for work.
My father works all the time.
Insecurity.
Green lawn.
Boss
Loss.
Boozer.
Loser.
Bob Black wrote *The Abolition of Work*
How can we better contract workforce management?
He can drink at work.
He drank himself out of work.
He worked himself to death.
Don't work too hard.
I work with a bunch of assholes.
They finally fired that bitch at work.

Where can I find work?
We can work it out.
We can work it out.
Life is very short
… and there's no ti i i i ime …
I'm taking the week off.
I'm retired.
I wrote my thesis on the leisure class in 20s Bavaria.
The professor laughed his ass off and then
he blew me from under that crappy work station.
Lumbar region.
What do you mean? You fucking work at Starbucks!
He went postal.
This shit's getting old.
I need you to make 300 of these an hour.
PR.
Fuck it! I quit.

Word is a Four-Letter Word
for Christian Bök and Kurt Schwitters

Word is a four-letter word
A Ordered Sorrowful Twit
Oh forget it

A Reworded Wistful Rotor
A hope for a city without a motor
A Reworded Sorrowful Tit
Not that you could get it
A Worldwide Roofer Strut
Well, take a look at that butt!
A Worldwide Roofer Trust
Surely such idiocy is a must

Not some old flippant re-utterance
NOTSOME OLIFFIPANTRY UTTER AUNTS
Neither some or none but new direction bleeding
Obedience Lending Writ
A sorrowful place to sit
Incredible Needing Two
Could be me, could be you?
Incredible Weeding Ton
A second without one?
Obedience Ginned Twirl
I've got just the girl!
Nee thirst summer nun-butt neuter,
erection bleeding

In the war, things were in terrible turmoil spoke
Schwitters
Terrible turmoil
A Lumberer Twirl Riot
A Libretti Ruler Worm
Whatsa matter?
See Americans Squirm
A Billet Writer Rumor
No insurance tumor.

new things had to be made out of the fragments,
Schwitters stated
new things fragments
Hangmen Wefts String
Dumb Police without Sting
Newsman Gent Frights
Deepfried chicken bites
Sharp talloned cockfights.
What a sight!

Word is a four-letter word
A Worldwide Otters Furor
A Worldwide Rooster Turf
Would you or would you not rape the smurf?
A Worldwide Terrors Tofu
A Worldwide Tortures For
A Worldwide Trouser Fort
Pass the potato salad.

Then when there is this over some four-letter:
What!
Oh, my God!
over some forletter werd,
Then when therwith is oversom forlet terword.
Then the we hen there withis oh versom for let
Err woe heard.

We heard, not comprehend or understand. No matter.
Wieherdnacht com prehendorough under stand nome at her.
comprehend understand
A Descended Hunt Mr Porn
A Drenched Tendons Rump
Jolly good pump pump.

Word is a four-letter word
A Worldwide Turrets Roof
A Twiddle Rooster Furrow
A Distorted Lower Furrow
A Dowdier Flutter Sorrow
A Dowdier Torturers Fowl
A Dowdier Torturers Wolf
A Dowdier Torturers Flow
Oh!?
Oh!?

Rot of this and that into something from within,
in dirty little unseen network of life that no sun
see until up and at them.
Rot of the sand that twosome thing from we
thin indie dirtily it looms, see?

Net woes work off lie if life
that nose unsees until opened
and datum.

Word is a four-letter word
A Deed Sorrowful Writ Rot
A Deed Furrows Twirl Root
A Deed Furrows Wilt Rotor
A Defiled Sorrow Trow Rut
A Refolded Writ Sour Trow
And how!

Not some flippant re-utterance.
Then when there with over sum four-let her wird.
Rot is this and that into something from within in
dirty, little unseen network of life that no sun
sees until up and atom.
Open-atom boom
Open it, ah!
Open, Adam. Boom!
Up Pen; a tomb.
I'm done.

Dead rot reassimilate
Dead rot reassimilate
Dead rot reassimilate
Dead
The rote reassembly simile up the rotary ass
I'm late.

Butt knew erect shunned
Mornin', Erect! New shine butt?

Isn't it glib?
Isn't it chic? wrote Bök

Isn't it Glib, chic?
Bitch Slicing It
Big Chitlins Tic
Bitch Icing Slit

Word is a four-letter word
A Soldiered Turf Trow Row
A Wielded Furor Worst Rot
A Wielded Fort Sorrow Rut
A Wielded Turf Rotor Rows
A Soldered Fruit Trow Row

Neither some or none but new direction pleading
for some four-letter word: word.
Direct pleading foursome-letterword:
Old flippant re-utterance
A Cad Referent Tiptop Null
A Cad Teleprinter Flop Nut
A Cad Teleprinter Loft Pun
A Cad Teleprinter Fun Plot

Dead rot reassimilate
Dead rot reassimilate
Dead rot reassimilate dEAd.

Ablutions

We might survive
kickball hegemony horsewhipped by Cossacks
nee goof troops on the loose pussy riot
drug combos that could prove you wrong.
A trash filled, crumbling, pothole-filled hellscape
to a lightning discovered shadow-dried tar,
caked around the rim.
Particleboard, plastic, chain restaurants, and traffic
of curiously long undergrads and creativity experts
cooking Native American Death penalty thesis ends
killing its own citizens.
The texture isn't the best
but still great in a winter salad
with two polar vortices.

Own your slave mentality
on a stick like a dilly bar.

No power means off the grid, man!
… and angry robots ruin fratboy logic
as five-gallon buckets skitter across the highways
to rest there until the wind
swept to the median
of jello.

We might survive.

Head will explode in 3 ... 2 ...1
Listen without visuals.
The lid off world ignoring
people who can afford to lose
a few brain cells

très attractive and invited to Nebula
Free tickets to all that will have them.
Please drink fish water
in the web of serene nevermore.

Creep

We've got a situation:
tilted swans are made of butter
magnets and insufferable twits.
Yuck it up at funerals. Nostalgia is for creeps.
Learn to love the little squiggles in the eyelids
and the murmurs in the heart.

But have you heard?
The go-to nerve syndrome
new virus and the ever
changing nature of slang
can be quite confusing
like the static
of a Berlusconi media
and your jittery morning
smile as birds hover
over your fevered bedhead.

It is the itch
under the sack
in your scalp
the facial tic
the stutter in your Mom's
hubbidahubudda Budhha
phone call now.

Yuck it up at funerals. Nostalgia is for creeps.
Learn to love the little squiggles in the eyelids
and the murmurs in the heart.

The blossoms aren't stunned
by schizophrenia
and the changes in weather;
nor are they confused
by the final connection
of the lock.
They react to the changes
with their own key,
but there's a girl
who's supposed to like unicorns
and all she wants is tequila
and maybe a sandwich
but all she gets is a story.

Never mind the history.
Ignorance is bliss is fear
is the right to be PC
is the right to be offended
by the mustard gas
in the formaldehyde
of the jar holding the idea
of Hitler's brain.

If you don't like the games,
the lines, then gallop
over them like John Lennon

Unicorn and rain piss
on the gods or as the wombat,
if you please, rough as a boar,
hard as a table
appearing cuddly.

Fuck on the water.
Get weird on a raft.
Surf on that wave
going over the dam.
Drink the blood
dripping from the damned.
Yuck it up at funerals. Nostalgia is for creeps.
Learn to love the little squiggles in the eyelids
and the murmurs in the heart.

Mind the outboard motor.
When the hearts of scar tissue
sings of hunger from your intestines
and Bob Kaufmann ceases
to believe in your dreams.

Blow the bass player.
Burn the books.
Buy drinks for the drummer.
Listen to your enemies.
They want to give you universal
access to anything
you can pay for with plastic.

Yuck it up at funerals. Nostalgia is for creeps.
Learn to love the little squiggles in the eyelids
and the murmurs in the heart.

Just as one would not show
one's hand to the father, that entity
that dealt it, felt it, held it, cherished it,
smelled it and knelt down in thanksgiving
for it, lest he thwart one's angst-felt wisdom;
so, too, do ignore the lists of the masses.
They are to be burning heaps,
steaming crocks of nothing
good, but for the ones
who conjured them up, wrote them down
and share the profits.

Kill the clouds and blot out
the sunshine if it omits desire
and stilts creativity and love.
Leave the world to sweat
and dream of ether.
Laugh at pain as it melts
or becomes more severe.

Eavesdrop, you Creep.
You will learn something.
She says, *Did we talk about the generator?*
He quotes the idiocy
only to misuse the word.

Grammar is for snobs.
Yuck it up at funerals. Nostalgia is for creeps.
Learn to love the little squiggles in the eyelids
and the murmurs in the heart.

Know your Mother while you teach
her to smuggle your conviction
to master agents of control
if you read this with your pants
on and the headphones turned up just a little
further than your buzz, dial the boss
and tell him it is for the candy-colored
bunions of your stagecoach Betty.
Tell him you desire butterfly dust
in your milk bottles in the morning.
Tell him. Tell him. Tell him there is no stain
without shouting and ape shit algelbra.
Tell him you love him. Set him free.

Stir the fear into the corn syrup
and watch the world waddle
in their muumuus.
If you have to engage further,
thank the world equally for pain
and giggles; thank the idea of the cosmos
as you do another migraine;
as you would an orgasm
that cripples;
or polio and the lack thereof
and the drivers in need
of dead pedestrians and rotting birds.

Yuck it up at funerals. Nostalgia is for creeps.
Learn to love the little squiggles in the eyelids
and the murmurs in the heart.

Tell the story about wellness falling
on the pilgrimage into nothingness
when never allowed something to peak
into the abyss
and the rain fell up the stairway
to find the love of a wombat
only to find that they are as hard as a table,
on the trail to moans.
Yuck it up at funerals. Nostalgia is for creeps.
Learn to love the little squiggles in the eyelids
and the murmurs in the heart.

We are a generation that consumes cultural
identities like locusts, but never digests any of them.
When you eat three then there are nine.
But is that true?
Try it sometime, then yell *HA! LOCUSTS!*

Generosity begat pain and deafness, sorrow.
Tweets and writhing
knew all the buttercups and the lids
of eyes fluttered upon a dismal mid-morning
as goats ate grass with dressing
on the side.

Yuck it up at funerals. Nostalgia is for creeps.
Tweets are crutches. Count the dead.
But if you need them, use them.
Know that sometimes
They are best meant for pretty birdies
and Satan brought home donuts
and it's Stanley Kubrick's fault
he typed; he tapped it into his device.
He quotes the idiocy.

... remember a time when a dyslexic
15-year old could perform a tonsillectomy
on a raging river with nothing but a bit
of quartz and a rotary phone
or live in a paper bag at the bottom
of a septic slaughterhouse
and not lose any sleep?
**The guy who made those cabinets
told me all about it.** Had the meter maid
delivered to his ulcer.
Still, it ain't over yet, but …

**I'm gonna miss my widget frag
my Don guy wag my wiggle in
the diggle of the wonkey lag
at Sunday do my jiggle jump
off the bridge in your slit,
you gape guy.
Poop in the atheist member
of mod flood, you Doufous!**

YOU DO FOR US! YOU MARY POPPINS WIGGLE WORM!!!
But, I won't share this except
to you, my confessor.

I HATE YOUR SHOES!!!!!
What are you doing there?
They create my fear.
Where do the toes go?

Surf on the wave
rushing across the dam.
Savor the blood gushing
from the damned.

Yuck it up at funerals. Nostalgia is for creeps.
Learn to love the little squiggles in the eyelids
and the murmurs in the heart.

Kleenex

Snotty sheriff, surely
you remember the sky is stingy
yet breaking water in a Montreal
spoon sticky wet stool and wasted eggs
revealing some fabulous white hexagonal tile
can't deny cheap poutine.
Labor, sore feet and beer tits
over the desperate attempts of hair spray
in spite of this hick dynasty
attitude leave creation
to some news pipe breaks in the grass
leaves.

Meanwhile, a matter
in the yuppies'
local tortellini sprinkled
with mounting corpses
and a need for maggots
when all we got is flies
deep to right
to the left of a hobbling
Dominican bouncing once
on the perfectly manicured
dilemma as the peasants dial
for fascist pizza rolls

or the homeless to transition
from bifocals to safety goggles
due to inclement bukkake
if I thought that there might
be any chance of the turtles
overtaking the snails.

Man's Crisis of Identity

A)
Button the lip but for a daft witticism
disinfecting citified minivan stories
stewed in knotted midsection oven
mittens telling the ancient news networks
with finger signals that fry the nothings
and insist incidents jumped the fence
dense but the dang boss (trafficker of snores)
in the picture was gone dripped off the smile
of the moneymaking pep in the step.
Fuck the criticism splatter jism
amidst nomads and their lawn furniture
sin and wetted with snorts from
a sweaty bottle of brown glass flew
over a confirmed tiny sister sitter
on the facelessness of the worker
who poured the gravity of labor and Santa
gave his lumbago to the slelves
yep—slave elves—
 not to mention tiny sirs and philanthropic
yuppies gifting guppies to a shark.

B)
Social lacing never quite hinders unseen
in the hump fields of the nevermind.
The stripping of hazy ids that couldn't begin
to lend abstraction to the expected
bocce ball precedent pretending
when that ditzy sixball's scent drips on a coerced ditz.
Or maybe the next hit spy rallying
for the invite of a possibility that the Moondaig
to drizzle Mussolini sugarnecktard on the rim
of your Grinch-hole low the cloud working
a lunch shift on Wednesday.
Weep easy. Weep long. Wipe the drips from your
gentle smirk.
Loosen the reins of your worksteady belch,
ye clodhoppers, ye Gophermenz.
Then, there came at last,
Old crayon, you grizzle,
from near the space needle of no syringe.
At the end of the day, his back aches
and she still smells like onions
muttering gravely into the whiskey
and half drunk ales.
Misery in the tea asks, *Why, mystery?*
at the rust in his socks.

C)
Ice Cream, a time void forcing you,
willing you to believe that you're an angel
to let that pouty dictator melt over the cone
to your cunning fingers of bliss
the hold the magic … oh! The magic!
The magic to render that mourning skeleton
into a man who no longer regrets
having butchered his mother's tongue
or letting you slip Cheerios into his guitar hole.
… AND SAVE A PRETZEL FOR THE GAS JETS!!

Wagon Wheel Cities are Annoying

Ezekiel saw the wheel in the sky
keep on turning
saw some window sniffin', banana baker in the local
asshole system with slutty, unwrapped hamburgers
saw some exclusive Bugs Bunny video
on at least two computers, a television,
in a reflective window pane.

Heard it on a DVD player plugged
into a gaming console.
Hid it in a wallet and a passport
with the angels cropped out by the bigoted,
redneck, woodtick, gun-toting, surly drinking,
Frisbee-chucking, conceal carry, info warrior,
ultra hippy, ultra city yuppie, over concerned gluten
free, suburban refugee, NPR contributing, pseudo liberal,
pseudo conservative, cowardly impotent assbags,
townie friends grasping at their *gun*
like a fucktard.

Sister Mary Soda Poppins cooked her tar
in a spoon over a candle.
Nodded off and dreamt about the whole
ball of wax and life with a good, cheap little guy
with asthma and a good heart.

Secretion accretion ejection depletion
osmosis and the thirst.
Lust hunger greed oozing the eternal slop
while Maggot Brain was finishing
 a swish and a thud and only caught
them running away.

Astro Pig

There was nothing left
of her but pubic hairs
I had yet to find
teetering on the toilet rim
upon the next sunrise.
Before noon,
by the time my carousel had stopped
on that fat holiday,
I discovered
a nonstop rage in children,
unemployed shortstops
as proofreaders
and the cigarette on the chair
more fizzle than sizzle
simultaneously preventing
and preparing for war.
Benson and Hedges
left as bait,
knocked and notorious
for changing my pulse.
Aries she was.
We made it for one night.
She called in two days.
Said it wasn't meant to be.
Something about the Pig being
incompatible with the Snake.

Spin Cycle

Pants looped after too many belts
don't promise success or bail free
waters under dirty skies.
Every mixture says don't when the balance
beam broke into a foxtrot just inside
the screen door where love splashes
on the rocks with the sand in the glass
falling faster than angels and stockbrokers
with sad suspenders oblivious to the spring
in the step of the dream-sick broad
in stained sweatpants cleaning out some boxes
for the rats to pray in the safety of their own
hunger wrapped in cloverleafs and buzzed
by choppers on the label of the hash can
is all I saw all day.

Shut up, will ya'?

The vicar's got a full count and a nasty
crease in his trousers.
His hitting streak is on the line and the laundry mat
could regurgitate on the way to actual soul music
in the busboy's shuffle.

Messy and Complicated and Riddled with Hypocrisy

A)
The monotheist says its purgatory
but its just life risen to the surface
like a grain of sand
lodged in a boil
on a mermaid's rump
seducing the helicopter
over the fire at a kettle corn kiosk versus
HOBBY LOBBY contraception
shadowing politics of the dollar whore
with the armadillo gun
remarkably obstinate for a dusty shaft of
of light for a pulp-loving hound
for a bandlegged ol' coot.

B)
Bands in the Wussy nation sparkling
dumpster diver files very affordably
but for Pakistani bouncy house
exalted by the conservative faithful
pop locking to a live swing band
all the more ghastly sand
blown away and the name
same but spelled a quip
a tagline a snappy headline

in wet dream dog food
and the blown spare tired
and homesick salty cardboard
no I in Cyclops
but you're not supposed to think about it
your fingers black from the newsprint

C)
Dead bunny tattoo
says commodify your dissent.
You feel like poop is good luck, goose.
Zeus raping a mythological swan
facilitating a good time twerk mpg
cake sedative for the opposite
defect when dog is nap interruptus
cause fingersnaps and lollygags whiskey
bong drams of 'tussin
and Kombucha tea prescribed
to Kerouac punished by Allah for not sitting
say polka dots are only
expression of internal stagnation

D)
Submission to the Sequoias who won't be
there in December air
conditioner with a butter knife
inner sword totem that did it straight
up but whoopin' Mr. Kitty

is probably cute at truck stops
on the secret recipe handshake kicked
outta the KFC after mauled by pitbulls
so they went to taco hell
morning lightning like a shot

E)
A good Christian drowns angry kitties
in a gunnysack snatched from the turtle
and flung in one graceful arc
into the burbling flume of the creek
we please we don't cry for me
Ike and Tina's salad don't take my disco
no place to air fuck ex-boyfriend bandana
in his right pocket, *purging*
of the unwanted medications derived from pig's
barf but diagnosed as faulty
because it shoots out of his head?
Searching for the Lard on Morgan Fard
Anything but gibbeted miscreants

F)
Human dignity, unborn infant life, and economic justice
on the back, you like something sleeping
in a cool house sworn off eventual
post-grunge power ballad pillow
that smells performance coming to grips
that his baby dropped the dog

bowl all like cocking onion rings sour
diction hear just one gun shot. Weird.
Ax the Fruit and fisters with: a picnic and a radio
instead of studying MTV
or millionaire camels in Detroit
tape knives to chickens
totally blowing up with photos only at head shops
mis-translated submissions healing profile
pictures paltry dwarves hashing
a portrait of Mojo playing the piano
opened a wormhole with no end
going to Bodi to seek
Riley's In C, erroneously in Ojai
leaves the somnambulist asking:
can Minimalists be Breeders?

Physics

If I told you what to imagine:
the tomato soup falling face first
croutons splattered from the gun
shot and the benevolent artist
coulda saved him if he would've just
pulled his wick out.
Dropped check. Smashed nose.
Mussolini's bastard child crying through the night
and the matadors telling
Rape jokes
Rape jokes
Rape jokes
about that artist who moved his feet wrong,
bought his Aunt lunch but couldn't save the soup.
They don't make salve for clutzy cunts like that,
they say in eclipsed moon speak ...
and then they drop six more mice
in the fryer and call it
cuisine.

If I could tell you to imagine that waste of sperm
you'd buy a tommy gun and mount it atop your minivan.
You'd tear HELL to the next box store, sure.
But you'd be screaming.
Oh, you'd be screaming.

Face first.
You're Dolly Parton CD skipping the mud.
You'd be ranting.
You'd be spreading those ivory thighs
for even four inches of dolemite
so you could keep the love in the honey.
Why wouldn't you?

Go Soothingly on the Grease Mud

I just saw the time of the text.
Vicky was at Denny's.
She likes it sticky.

Talking about that Turkish music
play teaches you
about the dangers of hyperbole.

Two down.
Tones and tropes
of the exterminator in a lullaby.

Fire a gun using a flute
as a suppressor.
Saw the time.

Jeremy Irons put almond
butter in case of fire.
Butterflies and zebras, too.

Fruit flies
became bees
and frogs with fuzz
aspirin in place of bananas.

Save money. Wash the dog.
She rolled in shit to teach you
the dangers of hyperbole.

Two artichokes abandoned on a crate
and always the tower, building
in a dystopian police state.
The braggart is flatulent.

The boat, the distant train and
a gun serving a Bibb Wedge
salad to a little man in a bolo.
You're head is going to be
on the ground. His feet are there
to kick it around.

You're better.
Scabs are the proof rock.
Nebulous are enemies.

Too late to duck you got drugged by a quack.
Got your panties in bunch
and you blame it on the wetbacks.

I ate my eggs
with caveman cutlery.
Scoff all you want.
The second-sacker is hard.

Loving loquacity.
Lapsing into logorrhea or
lisping like the imp.

The conversation was math
and its omnipotent stranglehold
on the sand.

I heard it.
Wasting the waves of hatred
on simple numbers.
Fraction-caused riots never
make the news.

Rolled in shit.
The Andalusian music of your fantasy
vibrates off your flimsy wrist.

Feeding alphabet soup to clerics
and engineers gets you to first base
without cleats.
Sometimes shit and motherhood
go
hand-in-hand.

Go soothingly on the grease mud
and where the skid demons lie.

Take your time.
The noisemaker's autonomy
is safe in the melee.

Fake puke cake in the break
room and sneak off to the racetrack.
Sure bet.

Butter in the race?
Make it a clarinet.
Eat your falafels out in the rain.

Jazzy sneezes and
nomenclature equate.
The lozenge lacks impetus.

To You, Cloudy Girl
The sky is a buffoon's attempt to conceal chance.
-Cassandra Stark Mele, *In Case of a Storm* 1995

Darkness and rain fall silently on rocks
where no brains understand.
Happiness is more than a mood, kid,
and a smile is less than bliss.
It's a facade like the sunshine
that only clears when vapor's gone.

The moon exists when it's hidden.
There is more to nature than weather.
We are fools to hang our consciousness
on such, thin, categorical tethers.
No revelation is there—no unseen truths,
just a continuing spray of babble.
Just remember, now please, don't despair.
Our spirits remain when no longer here.

If we wait, another mood will pass.
My lips eclipse will no longer persist
and my teeth will show like blue sky.
If you stop to consider this inevitability;
If you wait for it to happen;
If you listen and watch as the process unfolds;
Then your patience will be more
than any bottle could ever hold.

You will see that your waiting can carry you further
than any flittering flight of a fit.

So please try to find a hole
in the wall of balled up sounds
that tell you all is in your mind,
and completely dismiss the soul.

The mind is only a means.
Science is but a key.
But to find the way to unblemished truth
we must wait indefinitely.
For if we rush past all the clues
towards an end for which we lust,
we'll miss the meaning of every connection
as gods smile while we wait for the bus.

Sometimes I Work in a Grandiose Castle

standing on clouds of epiphanies
the rush of the hungry and the damned
washed away
I stop and look out the aged
windows to the world
Wonder what its like to look
in at the lights
the calmly dining
public
Them
free from the streets
locked away from danger
Hunger
and the mad rush for goods

Out there snow
falls silently
on barren branches that
never bear fruit
but only sticks of leaves
void of nourishment
only serving to break
up the asphalt beds
of the commuting damned

A vagrant few pass through alleys
behind the blockaded forts
of the captains of industry
and I am safe to observe
in the warmth of perusal
under pillars and beams
of long since slaughtered cedars

I imagine that I am seated
near one of those small saplings
out there
In a simple wooden chair
sipping cheap bourbon
or other distilled and warming spirits
The wind and cold no challenge
as I look in and see
myself
with scorn
standing behind my altar
of refined leisure
each sip melts the hatred

Until another order for urgency
makes itself known
in the form of shrieking
and harried voices
both human and electronic
To the clacking of credit

cards on the bar
My feet turn to glass
as the clouds
on which I was wondering
shoot needles of sleet into my mind

The calm faces turn
to those of ghouls
with gnashing teeth
and hungry, blood-sucking
souls
the chupacabra have come

I am not sweating
The small stuff
I'm bleeding minutiae
out my eyes
But
It is time to make due
until I can wonder why
such precious still moments
are few

Or moments like these
when I can
get them down
out of a fuzzed
attic space

Just now, I've returned from a quick
few drags on the back porch
during a break
from Winter
The birds are chirping stupidly
as a church bell rings
but a generator is growling
at the end of an alley
from a building being rehabbed
in the name of real estate
Renovation
Commerce
and the good of the city

I know I'm lucky to have
such easy disturbances
like yipping schnauzers
clomping neighbors
on wooden steps
and the banging and clanging
of carpentry
free from Jesus

But I can't help to feel
their encroachment as threatening
while a taxi's horn blares
for the fat lady
to waddle down for her ride
to somewhere else
and the clock catches my eye

Soon I'll be returning to the trenches
to fight off these fears of aging
To loosen myself
from the nooses of debt
to free myself
for more easy moments
as the future yawns uncertainly
Stretching its jaws for its next meal
languid and waiting
for its soon-to-come
easy gruel of we
the restless
on a Saturday night
Easing ourselves down
into the belly of the beast
A mad rush
for more of the good, dirty
funnish Hell
our substance used
to feed the cosmic slop.

Headbutt Baby

It was 4:15 when Jim ordered another glass of lager
and groaned.
The dim light crept across the room
hesitantly.
Unable to conquer dusty shadows
and the lethargy of a Tuesday afternoon,
it lent a quiet beauty to the brown
and green bottles and the gray eyes
and stubble of the men who sat
suckling at the glass tit
in the corner that blurted a game show.
Oh, Christ! Give it up, Kid! You're a dick!
screeched the bartender, impatient
with a contestant's hesitant answers.
Sucking on a swizzle stick, he turned to Jim.
What's got you today, Jimbo?
Jim moved his left shoulder in a forward shrug
of a circle and lifted the arm that was hanging
in a sling.
Oh...Well...I really did it this time.
Not sure where I'll be sleeping tonight, but I've gone
from the bed to the couch
and might be out on the street
after yesterday.

Aw shit. Let's have it. What happened this time?
the bartender answered.
*Well ... she didn't feel like cooking the other day
and we had just got our check, so I said,
why don't I go over to Torrino's and get a pizza pie?
So, I ride my bike over there and they were busy,
really busy, so I popped in to see Alice
over at the Drip Drop.
You know—next door?
So I got to talkin' to her and in walks
this young couple
and hey, lemme tell ya' the guy was little
squirrely, but this gal he had with 'im
was a doe-eyed slice of heaven.
He was all tied up with some conversation
on his cell phone, so she and I started talking.
Anyway, he keeps on babbling on
and I do an end-around and sit down
on the other side of her and she starts
asking me about this and that
And telling me about her schoolwork
and her job at the hospital
and then he drops his phone to his chest and orders three
double shots of Jagermeister.*

Oh shit, came a chorus from the other five
regulars at the bar. *Here we go.*

So he gets off the phone eventually
and seems to be upset about something
and then there is another round:
three double-shots of Jagermeister.
I need to leave soon after that,
but they said NO,
here
order your pizza
on our phone and you can pick it up
in 25 minutes while you finish your beer.
Beer?! I said.
… and here came a little glass of that Russian stout
they have over there.
Alice kinda gave me a look and a wink
and slid it on over
and you know my grandmother used to cook
with that stuff and would drink
it in the morning around Christmas,
so I'm not afraid.
But, boy, it all hit me pretty good
and I finally excused myself,
went to the can
and snuck out the back screen door.
So, I got the pie and got it on the back of my bike
and I get up on the thing and everything is O.K.!
I'm cruising north and there isn't much traffic
and the breeze is feeling good.
But, you know, I got to Randolph there

*and the light is yellow and there is no way
I'm gonna make it,
so I have to stop.
That's a busy intersection you know?
Well, there's this young gal with her baby
in a stroller and I'm tying my shoe
and then the light turns green
and I kinda push off the curb, but I feel
myself going and the front
wheel is wobbling and then
I went down.*

All heads turned to look at Jim.

*At first, I was afraid that I was gonna
run into the mother from the back,
but I missed her. I still dumped the bike
though and then I kinda rolled
and you know what?*

What, Dummy?!! chimed the choir.

*Well, I landed and then my head hit
one of the wheels of the stroller
and the wheel came off
and the stroller tipped over
and I was lying there in the street
face-to-face with the baby*

*and it had these incredible
blue eyes.
These really, beautiful, bright, blue eyes.*

*Anyway, the pizza was all over the ground,
but the baby was all right
and the lady was a little startled,
but nice.*

*You know,
people are really nice.*

Jim looked around at blank stares.

*All right, I gotta go.
What do I owe ya?*

As he swung the door open
a light rain fell
and Jim saw several pigeons dart
down off a building and
swoop up under
a parked church bus.

Vision or ...

The movements and sounds
of the night
or the stillness of each
day is a lie,
lying in each life
awake to attention and
numbness to the lines
like pigeons all in a row.
There are no lines
no separation
when you feel alive.
Field of vision
lift of feathers
soaring towards an easy
meal with talons sharp.
Music in each movement
a click, a tap, a far off cry
and the silence of a passing tick
tock free of an urge to
scratch the itch.
Escape the bossman.
Flit freely.
Swing away.
Glide and grin.
Laugh at the gunman.

Time peace delusion
butts up to the psychosis
of learning the truth
and the battle,
the struggle
to believe
you have been
here before.

… and there are no lines
no separation
when you feel alive.
When you remember
to breathe.

If
you
can.

Slick

The bird of paradise knows no
no-fly zone and there is no potion
too potent to the surrealist;
thus profit the hunter and the pusher.
Still, Uncle Dave's convinced he's got
a shot with the wet nurse and her soapy
strokes until she slows the drip.
The strap of any purse
won't deny the carefree snatcher
oblivious to the ubiquitous cams
like a forearm shiver
or a slapstick banana peel
on a day when the plankton
are plentiful for the great fish
and the finned mammals
while the lefty lays one down the middle
to the tater king who whiffs
on the next two dipping junk balls
and won't get action
from the starlets and doesn't care,
his dreams buried in the depths of the mitt
and his shrunken nuts.
When the wet blades give to the swift
sickle of the harvester who lost
his lumbago in the grace of an efficient arc

the news networks are on picnic
their 12-point lines carrying the sweet
smell of clean sheets in the lilac breezes
that yearn to carry the laundress' perspiration
to the docks
where the slime of fornicating slipper snails
know no laws of friction,
just the inevitable death
at the bottom of the orgy
and the larger males
that take their place as females,
sequentially hermaphroditic
and not likely to inbreed and weather
Old Testament judgment
only to find their post-coital demise
despite shells and iron-deficient
waifs still squeamish about texture
slicker than a finger
in the honey.

The Chainsaw Says *Get Up!*

A crisp and explosive morning
does not meet well with blasé.
Chainsaws and the digital rings
of telephones; stomping of feet
and slamming of doors; grinding
and whining of street-cleaning
trucks do not meet well with blasé.
They spell the absence of sacred awakening.
Now, the sunshine has set the sky
to flames and licks at the edges
of living space.
Sleep is impossible
amidst such industry,
but now even nature
demands arousal.

Chainsaws, leaf blowers
and lawn mowers in *quiet*
neighborhoods replace gunshots and thunder
until the whole thing meets bombs.

The saxophonist can't sleep and now you are restless,
but when the man in the coveralls
puts down his hand-held engine
and the jazzman hears the humming

of his nervous system
to the ticking of the clock,
the sunshine through the partially
open curtains is enough to relax
venomous vim and dash all hopes
of ever doing anything about it
as a child screams on a nearby asphalt
playground, a delivery truck
roars the wrong way towards a dead end
and the church bell rings nine.

Out of the Tree

In the morning, on a day
when I don't have to work,
I climb trees and nibble
on bits of pecans.
I am a squirrel.

In my mind, I put shoe dust
into carburetors and yell
into my heart,
DO SOMETHING FANTASTIC!!!
then whisper
you're O.K. you're O.K

I get out of the tree.
There are more nuts
on the ground where I belong.

Turns out this bicycle
has propellers and voices
that sing and my legs
are not tools, but wings.

Take a look
in the mirror
and a bird appears
and suggests
Man, you are crazy.

Go back to bed.

Brett Lars Underwood is a bartender and a gadabout who writes, promotes and produces happenings and mishaps in St. Louis. Once upon a time, he co-published a 'zine entitled *Lick My Squaggle Noose, Clam Tick*. He penned Zen koans for *The Riverfront Times* and *St. Louis Magazine* as well as *Curator*. He has performed in back rooms, backyards, ball rooms, barrooms, basements, coffee houses, courtyards, galleries, museums, rock venues and taverns. His verse and riddles have been published by *The Bicycle Review, 52nd City, The Subterranean, Bad Shoe* and included in *Flood Stage: An Anthology of Saint Louis Poets* and *The Gasconade Review presents 39 Feet And Rising.* He unleashed *Sunlit Insult,* his first chapbook, in 2011 and *Its Bush Lent Subtle Hints* in October, 2013. He can be reached at brettlarsunderwood@gmail.com

This project was made possible, in part, by generous support from the Osage Arts Community.

Osage Arts Community provides temporary time, space and support for the creation of new artistic works in a retreat format, serving creative people of all kinds — visual artists, composers, poets, fiction and nonfiction writers. Located on a 152-acre farm in an isolated rural mountainside setting in Central Missouri and bordered by ¾ of a mile of the Gasconade River, OAC provides residencies to those working alone, as well as welcoming collaborative teams, offering living space and workspace in a country environment to emerging and mid-career artists. For more information, visit us at www.oac.com